Everything Is Figure-outable

outable

THE WORKBOOK

Disclaimer

This workbook is intended to be an educational resource and self-help guide. It is not intended to be a substitute for professional counseling or therapy. If you are struggling with any of the topics covered in this workbook, please seek help from a qualified professional. The author has made every effort to ensure the accuracy of the information in this workbook, but some errors or omissions may be present. The author is not responsible for any negative consequences that may arise from the use of this workbook.

LESSONS IN THIS WORKBOOK:

Chapter 1: All Problems Are Figureoutable

Chapter 2: Belief Systems

Chapter 3: The Magic of Thinking Big

Chapter 4: Starting Before You're Ready

Chapter 5: Excuses Begone!

Chapter 6: Progress, Not Perfection

Chapter 7: How to Develop Grit

Chapter 8: The Imposter Syndrome

Chapter 9: How to Get Anything You Want

Chapter 10: Everything is Figureoutable at Work

Chapter 11: Everything is Figureoutable in Love

Chapter 12: Everything is Figureoutable with Health

Chapter 13: Everything is Figureoutable with Money

Chapter 14: Everything is Figureoutable with Time

Chapter 1: All Problems Are Figureoutable

Lesson 1:

Embracing the Figureoutable Mindset

Problem-Solution Reflection: Think about a recent problem or challenge you faced. Write down the problem, how it made you feel, and your initial thoughts on solving it. Then, reflect on how you can apply the principle of "Everything is figureoutable" to find solutions. Write down at least three potential solutions.

_____

_____

_____

_____

_____

_____

_____

_____

_____

_____

_____

_____

_____

_____

_____

_____

_____

_____

_____

_____

_____

_____

_____

_____

Empowerment Affirmations: Create a list of empowering affirmations related to the principle. For example, "I have the power to overcome any obstacle," or "I can find solutions to challenges." Write down these affirmations and repeat them daily to reinforce your belief in your problem-solving abilities.

_____

_____

_____

_____

_____

_____

_____

_____

_____

_____

_____

_____

_____

_____

_____

_____

_____

_____

_____

_____

_____

_____

Past Successes: Recall a situation from your past where you success-fully solved a challenging problem. Write a detailed account of that experience, highlighting the steps you took and the mindset you had. Use this as a reminder that you have a track record of figuring things out.

Lesson 2:

Overcoming Mental Blocks

Identify Limiting Beliefs: Reflect on any limiting beliefs or negative thought patterns that have held you back from tackling challenges. Write down at least three of these beliefs. Then, challenge each one by providing evidence to the contrary.

Fear Assessment: List any fears or anxieties that have hindered your problem-solving in the past. Write down how these fears make you feel and the specific challenges they've created. Explore strategies for confronting and overcoming these fears.

_____

_____

_____

_____

_____

_____

_____

_____

_____

_____

_____

_____

_____

_____

_____

_____

_____

_____

_____

_____

_____

_____

Obstacle Visualization: Visualize a significant obstacle you currently face. Write a detailed description of the obstacle and how it appears in your mind. Now, create a vivid mental image of yourself successfully navigating and overcoming that obstacle. Use this visualization to boost your confidence.

Lesson 3:

Cultivating Relentless Belief

Daily Challenge Log: Create a "Daily Challenge Log" where you record one challenge or problem you encounter each day. Write down your initial feelings and thoughts about solving it. After the challenge is resolved, document the solution and how you felt afterward. This practice reinforces your problem-solving mindset.

Success Journal: Start a "Success Journal" to record instances when you successfully solve problems or face challenges. Write about the problem, the actions you took, and the positive outcomes. Regularly review this journal to remind yourself of your problem-solving abilities.

_____

_____

_____

_____

_____

_____

_____

_____

_____

_____

_____

_____

_____

_____

_____

_____

_____

_____

_____

_____

_____

Mentor or Role Model Inspiration: Identify a mentor, role model, or someone you admire who embodies the figureoutable mindset. Write down their key qualities and principles they live by. Use their example as inspiration to further develop your relentless belief in solving problems.

Chapter 2: Belief Systems

Lesson 1:

Reflecting on Belief Systems

Belief System Inventory: List five core beliefs you hold about yourself, your abilities, or the world around you. Write down where these beliefs came from and whether they are empowering or limiting. Reflect on how they have influenced your actions and outcomes.

_____

_____

_____

_____

_____

_____

_____

_____

_____

_____

_____

_____

_____

_____

_____

_____

_____

_____

_____

_____

_____

_____

_____

_____

_____

_____

_____

_____

Belief Exploration: Select one limiting belief that has held you back in the past. Write a detailed account of how this belief has affected your decisions and actions. Include specific situations where it hindered your progress.

_____

_____

_____

_____

_____

_____

_____

_____

_____

_____

_____

_____

_____

_____

_____

_____

_____

_____

_____

_____

_____

_____

_____

_____

Belief Transformation Plan: Choose one of the limiting beliefs you've identified and create a plan to transform it into an empowering belief. Write down the new belief you want to adopt and at least three actions or strategies you can use to reinforce this new belief.

_____

_____

_____

_____

_____

_____

_____

_____

_____

_____

_____

_____

_____

_____

_____

_____

_____

_____

_____

_____

_____

_____

_____

_____

_____

_____

_____

_____

_____

Lesson 2:

Challenging and Changing Beliefs

Belief Challenge Journal: Start a journal where you record instances when you catch yourself thinking or acting based on limiting beliefs. Write down the belief, the situation, and how it held you back. Then, brainstorm alternative beliefs or perspectives to challenge the limiting one.

Belief Evolution Timeline: Create a timeline of your life, noting significant events or experiences that may have contributed to the development of your beliefs. Write down how each event affected your beliefs, whether positively or negatively. This exercise helps you understand the origins of your beliefs.

_____

_____

_____

_____

_____

_____

_____

_____

_____

_____

_____

_____

_____

_____

_____

_____

_____

_____

_____

_____

_____

_____

Affirmation Development: Choose one empowering belief you want to reinforce. Write down affirmations or positive statements related to this belief. Use these affirmations daily to counteract and replace any lingering limiting beliefs.

Lesson 3:

Reframing with "Wouldn't it be great if...?"

Limiting Belief Transformation: Select a specific limiting belief you want to reframe. Write it down. Then, complete the sentence: "Wouldn't it be great if..." with a positive and empowering statement that counteracts the limiting belief. Repeat this exercise daily to shift your perspective.

Visualization Exercise: Visualize a scenario where your reframed belief is fully realized. Write a detailed description of this scenario, including how it looks, feels, and the positive outcomes it leads to. Use this visualization as a mental exercise to reinforce the new belief.

_____

_____

_____

_____

_____

_____

_____

_____

_____

_____

_____

_____

_____

_____

_____

_____

_____

_____

_____

_____

_____

_____

_____

Action Plan: Develop an action plan that aligns with your reframed belief. Write down specific steps or actions you can take to live in accordance with this new belief. Commit to implementing these steps in your daily life to solidify the positive belief.

_____

_____

_____

_____

_____

_____

_____

_____

_____

_____

_____

_____

_____

_____

_____

_____

_____

_____

_____

_____

_____

_____

_____

_____

_____

Chapter 3:
The Magic of Thinking Big

Lesson 1:

Setting Audacious Goals

Big Dreams Brainstorm: Reflect on your life goals and dreams. Write down at least three significant goals that you've always wanted to achieve but may have considered too ambitious. These should be "big dreams" that excite and challenge you.

Goal Visualization: Select one of your big dreams from the list.
Write a detailed visualization of what achieving that dream would
look like. Include sensory details, emotions, and specific outcomes.
Visualization can help solidify your belief in the goal.

Goal Breakdown: Take your chosen big dream and break it down into smaller, manageable milestones or steps. Write down these milestones, along with deadlines or target dates for achieving them. Breaking the goal into parts makes it more actionable.

Lesson 2:

Applying the 10x Rule

Goal Expansion: Review one of the goals you've set in the previous activity. Apply the "10x Rule" by imagining what it would take to make that goal ten times bigger. Write down how the goal and its impact would change if it were ten times larger.

Stretching Your Efforts: Identify one area of your life where you've been holding back or playing it safe. Write down at least three ways you can stretch your efforts in that area to align with the 10x mind-set. These actions should push you beyond your comfort zone.

Bold Action Plan: Choose one bold action related to your big dream that you can take immediately. Write down the action, a deadline, and the potential benefits and risks. Implementing bold actions is key to making significant progress.

Lesson 3:

Embracing Discomfort

Fear Exploration: Reflect on any fears or hesitations you have about pursuing your big dreams. Write down these fears and the specific situations or obstacles that trigger them. Acknowledging your fears is the first step in overcoming them.

Comfort Zone Map: Create a visual representation of your comfort zone, depicting the boundaries of what feels safe and familiar. Write down at least three actions or steps that would push you outside this comfort zone in pursuit of your big dreams.

Growth Reflection: Write a letter to your future self, looking back on your journey toward your big dreams. Describe how embracing discomfort and taking bold actions has contributed to your growth and success. Use this letter as a source of motivation.

Chapter 4:
Starting Before You're Ready

Lesson 1:

Embracing Imperfect Action

Imperfect Action Plan: Identify a specific goal or project you've been hesitating to start because you feel unprepared. Write down the goal and list the steps or actions required to begin. Commit to taking the first step within a specific timeframe, even if it feels imperfect.

Fear Identification: Reflect on the fears or self-doubt that have prevented you from starting projects in the past. Write down at least three of these fears and how they have hindered your progress. Acknowledging these fears is the first step in overcoming them.

Action vs. Perfection: Write a comparison between the potential outcome of taking imperfect action and the outcome of waiting for the "perfect" moment. Include both the benefits and drawbacks of each approach. Use this analysis to motivate yourself to start before you're ready.

Lesson 2:

Learning Through Action

Reflect on Past Experiences: Think about a situation in your life where you took action despite feeling unprepared. Write down the details of that experience, including what you learned and any positive outcomes. This reflection highlights the value of imperfect action.

Action Feedback Loop: Choose a small project or task that you can start immediately. Write down your initial goals and expectations. As you take action, periodically document your progress, challenges, and insights. This exercise creates a feedback loop for continuous improvement.

Growth Journal: Begin a "Growth Journal" where you record the lessons, skills, and personal growth you gain from taking imperfect action. Write down the positive changes and new knowledge you acquire through your experiences.

_____

_____

_____

_____

_____

_____

_____

_____

_____

_____

_____

_____

_____

_____

_____

_____

_____

_____

_____

_____

_____

_____

_____

_____

_____

_____

Lesson 3:

Overcoming Fear and Self-Doubt

Fear Confrontation: List three specific projects or goals you've been hesitating to start due to fear or self-doubt. Write down the main fears associated with each one. Next, challenge these fears with evidence of your past achievements and capabilities.

_____

_____

_____

_____

_____

_____

_____

_____

_____

_____

_____

_____

_____

_____

_____

_____

_____

_____

_____

_____

_____

_____

Self-Doubt Counteraction: Create a list of empowering affirmations and positive self-talk statements related to your abilities. Write them down and use them as a daily reminder to counteract self-doubt when it arises.

Accountability Partner: Identify someone in your life who can serve as an accountability partner for your goals. Write down the goals you want to pursue and share them with this person. Regular check-ins with your accountability partner can motivate you to start before you're ready.

Chapter 5:
Excuses Begone!

Lesson 1:

Recognizing and Eliminating Excuses

Excuse Awareness: Reflect on a recent situation where you made an excuse for not taking action or achieving a goal. Write down the excuse and the impact it had on your progress. Acknowledging excuses is the first step to eliminating them.

Excuse Inventory: Create an "Excuse Inventory" by listing common excuses you've used in different areas of your life (e.g., career, health, relationships). Write down the excuses you've noticed yourself using most frequently. Recognizing patterns can help you address them.

_____

_____

_____

_____

_____

_____

_____

_____

_____

_____

_____

_____

_____

_____

_____

_____

_____

_____

_____

_____

_____

_____

Excuse Elimination Plan: Choose one of the excuses from your inventory and develop a plan to eliminate it. Write down alternative actions you can take when faced with this excuse in the future. Commit to implementing these alternatives and holding yourself accountable.

_____

_____

_____

_____

_____

_____

_____

_____

_____

_____

_____

_____

_____

_____

_____

_____

_____

_____

_____

_____

_____

_____

Lesson 2:

The 10x Life Inventory Exercise

Goal Evaluation: Write down a significant life goal or aspiration you have. Next, apply the "10x Life Inventory" exercise by listing actions or choices that have held you back from achieving this goal. Reflect on how these actions differ from the actions of someone who has achieved a similar goal.

Action Comparison: Select a goal from your previous exercise and list ten specific actions you could take to move closer to it. Compare these actions to the excuses you've identified in your "Excuse Inventory." Write down how each action counters an excuse.

_____

_____

_____

_____

_____

_____

_____

_____

_____

_____

_____

_____

_____

_____

_____

_____

_____

_____

_____

_____

_____

_____

_____

_____

Accountability Partner: Choose a friend, family member, or colleague to serve as an accountability partner. Share your goals and excuses with them. Commit to regular check-ins where you update them on your progress and hold yourself accountable for eliminating excuses.

Lesson 3:

Taking Responsibility for Your Choices

Choice Reflection: Write a reflection on the role of personal choices in your life. Consider how choices, both big and small, have contributed to your current circumstances. Take responsibility for the impact of these choices, whether positive or negative.

_____

_____

_____

_____

_____

_____

_____

_____

_____

_____

_____

_____

_____

_____

_____

_____

_____

_____

_____

_____

_____

_____

_____

_____

Responsibility Statement: Craft a personal responsibility statement that reflects your commitment to taking ownership of your life. Write it in the first person, present tense (e.g., "I take full responsibility for my choices and actions"). Repeat this statement daily to reinforce your mindset.

Accountability Journal: Start an "Accountability Journal" where you record daily choices and actions related to your goals. Write down moments when you successfully resisted making excuses and took proactive steps toward your objectives. Reflect on how this accountability journal keeps you on track.

Chapter 6: Progress, Not Perfection

Lesson 1:

Embracing Imperfection and Progress

Perfectionism Self-Assessment: Reflect on situations in your life where perfectionism has held you back or caused unnecessary stress. Write down at least three examples. Recognizing these instances is essential for change.

Progress-Perfection Comparison: Choose a specific goal or project you're currently working on. Write down the ideal outcome you'd achieve with perfection and compare it to the progress you've made so far. Embrace the idea that progress is more valuable than unattainable perfection.

Imperfect Action Plan: Select a goal or task you've been hesitant to start due to the fear of imperfection. Write down the first step you can take to move forward. Commit to taking this imperfect action within a specified timeframe.

Lesson 2:

Cultivating a Progress Mindset

Progress Mindset Affirmations: Create a list of affirmations that reinforce a progress-oriented mindset (e.g., "I value the journey of progress," or "Mistakes are opportunities for growth"). Write down these affirmations and repeat them daily to shift your focus.

Failure as Feedback: Recall a recent mistake or setback you experienced in pursuit of a goal. Write down what you learned from that experience and how it contributed to your growth. Reframe mistakes as valuable feedback.

_____

_____

_____

_____

_____

_____

_____

_____

_____

_____

_____

_____

_____

_____

_____

_____

_____

_____

_____

_____

_____

_____

_____

_____

Progress Journal: Start a "Progress Journal" where you document daily or weekly achievements and steps taken toward your goals. Write down your feelings of accomplishment and track your progress over time. This journal serves as a motivational tool.

Lesson 3:

Consistent Effort and Learning

Goal Breakdown: Take one of your long-term goals and break it down into smaller, more manageable milestones or tasks. Write down these milestones along with deadlines or target dates. Focus on the incremental progress needed to achieve the larger goal.

_____

_____

_____

_____

_____

_____

_____

_____

_____

_____

_____

_____

_____

_____

_____

_____

_____

_____

_____

_____

_____

_____

Feedback Loop: Choose a skill or area of improvement you're currently working on. Write down specific actions or activities you can engage in to develop that skill. Create a feedback loop by recording your progress and adjustments as you go.

Growth Mindset Reflection: Reflect on the difference between a fixed mindset (focused on achieving perfection) and a growth mindset (focused on progress and learning). Write about how adopting a growth mindset can benefit your personal and professional development.

Chapter 7:
How to Develop Grit

Lesson 1:

Recognizing the Importance of Grit

Personal Grit Assessment: Reflect on your current projects, goals, or aspirations. Write down examples where you've demonstrated grit, showing both passion and perseverance. Acknowledging your past grit is a powerful motivator.

Success Stories: Research and identify individuals who have achieved remarkable success in their fields through grit. Write down their stories, focusing on the challenges they faced and how their determination and persistence led to their accomplishments. Use these stories as sources of inspiration.

_____

_____

_____

_____

_____

_____

_____

_____

_____

_____

_____

_____

_____

_____

_____

_____

_____

_____

_____

_____

_____

_____

_____

Grit Manifesto: Create a "Grit Manifesto" by writing a statement that reflects your commitment to cultivating grit. Include your willingness to face setbacks and stay passionate about your goals. Read this manifesto regularly to reinforce your grit mindset.

Lesson 2:

Cultivating Grit in Practice

Goal Commitment Plan: Choose a significant long-term goal you want to achieve. Write down your reasons for pursuing this goal, emphasizing the passion and commitment behind it. List potential obstacles or setbacks you may encounter and how you plan to overcome them.

Obstacle Overcoming Strategy: Select one of the obstacles you identified in the previous activity. Write down specific strategies or actions you can take to overcome this obstacle. Focus on resilience and perseverance in the face of challenges.

_____

_____

_____

_____

_____

_____

_____

_____

_____

_____

_____

_____

_____

_____

_____

_____

_____

_____

_____

_____

_____

_____

Grit Routine: Develop a daily or weekly routine that emphasizes grit. Write down tasks or activities that align with your long-term goals and require consistent effort. Use this routine to reinforce your commitment to grit and perseverance.

Lesson 3:

Implementing the "One More Thing" Principle

Identify Challenges: List three challenging situations or goals you're currently working on. Write down the specific obstacles or difficulties you've encountered in each case.

"One More Thing" Action Plan: Apply the "One More Thing" principle to each of the challenges you've identified. Write down one additional action or step you can take in each situation to push through the difficulties. Commit to taking these extra steps.

_____

_____

_____

_____

_____

_____

_____

_____

_____

_____

_____

_____

_____

_____

_____

_____

_____

_____

_____

_____

_____

_____

_____

_____

_____

Reflection on Grit Growth: After implementing the "One More Thing" principle in various situations, reflect on your experiences. Write about how this additional effort affected your progress and mindset. Identify any shifts in your ability to persevere and stay passionate about your goals.

_____

_____

_____

_____

_____

_____

_____

_____

_____

_____

_____

_____

_____

_____

_____

_____

_____

_____

_____

_____

_____

_____

_____

_____

Chapter 8:
The Imposter Syndrome

Lesson 1:

Acknowledging and Addressing Self-Doubt

Imposter Syndrome Self-Reflection: Reflect on moments in your life when you've experienced imposter syndrome. Write down the specific situations, your feelings of self-doubt, and any actions or decisions influenced by these feelings.

Self-Doubt Inventory: Create a list of common self-doubts or negative thoughts you've had about your abilities, skills, or accomplishments. Write down how these thoughts have impacted your confidence and actions.

Positive Affirmations: Develop a list of positive affirmations that counteract self-doubt. Write them down and make it a daily practice to recite these affirmations to boost your self-confidence and self-worth.

Lesson 2:

Embracing Imposter Syndrome as a Growth Opportunity

Success Stories with Imposter Syndrome: Research and compile success stories of well-known individuals who have openly discussed experiencing imposter syndrome. Write down their names, achievements, and how they turned their self-doubt into motivation.

Growth Plan with Imposter Syndrome: Choose a specific area of personal or professional growth you want to pursue. Write down your goals, acknowledging the potential imposter syndrome-related challenges you might face. Develop strategies to address these challenges and continue your growth journey.

_____

_____

_____

_____

_____

_____

_____

_____

_____

_____

_____

_____

_____

_____

_____

_____

_____

_____

_____

_____

_____

_____

Imposter Syndrome Journal: Start an "Imposter Syndrome Journal" to record instances when you feel self-doubt creeping in. Write about the thoughts and emotions you experience, but also include actions you take to counteract them. This journal helps you track your progress in overcoming imposter syndrome.

Lesson 3:

Finding Strength in Shared Experiences

Imposter Syndrome Community: Seek out or create a community of individuals who openly discuss and share their experiences with imposter syndrome. Write down the names or resources of communities, books, or articles that provide support and encouragement.

Mentor or Role Model Reflection: Identify a mentor or role model who has faced imposter syndrome in their journey to success. Write about their influence on your life and how their experiences inspire you to navigate your own imposter syndrome.

Imposter Syndrome Letter: Write a letter to your future self, reflecting on your journey to overcome imposter syndrome. Describe the progress you've made and the lessons you've learned. Use this letter as a source of motivation during moments of self-doubt.

Chapter 9: How to Get Anything You Want

Lesson 1:

Goal Breakdown and Prioritization

Goal Breakdown: Choose a specific goal you want to achieve. Write down the main components or steps required to accomplish this goal. Break it down into smaller, manageable tasks or milestones.

Prioritization Matrix: Create a prioritization matrix by listing all your current goals or aspirations. Categorize them into "Must-Have," "Should-Have," and "Nice-to-Have" goals. Write down the reasons why each goal falls into its respective category.

_____

_____

_____

_____

_____

_____

_____

_____

_____

_____

_____

_____

_____

_____

_____

_____

_____

_____

_____

_____

_____

_____

_____

_____

Goal Action Plan: Select one of your "Must-Have" goals. Write a detailed action plan that includes specific tasks, deadlines, and resources needed. Prioritize these tasks based on their importance and start with the most critical ones.

Lesson 2:

Maintaining Focus and Consistency

Focus Declaration: Write a statement that reflects your commitment to maintaining focus on your goals. Include specific behaviors or habits you will adopt to stay on track. Read this declaration daily to reinforce your focus.

Consistency Tracker: Create a "Consistency Tracker" where you record daily or weekly actions related to your goals. Write down the tasks you complete and rate your consistency. Use this tracker as a visual tool to monitor your progress.

Obstacle Analysis: Identify potential obstacles or distractions that could hinder your focus and consistency. Write down strategies to overcome each obstacle, and include contingency plans for when you encounter setbacks.

Lesson 3:

Using the "Three Bs" Manifestation Approach

Belief Enhancement: Write a list of affirmations or empowering beliefs related to your goals. These beliefs should reflect your unwavering confidence in achieving them. Repeat these affirmations daily to reinforce your belief.

Behavioral Alignment: Review your daily behaviors and routines. Write down any behaviors that align with your goals and those that may hinder your progress. Develop a plan to adjust your behaviors to better support your desired outcomes.

Business Strategy: If your goals involve business or financial success, outline a high-level strategy to achieve them. Write down key milestones, partnerships, or revenue targets. This strategy serves as a roadmap to manifesting your desires.

Chapter 10:
Everything is Figureoutable at Work

Lesson 1:

Applying the "Everything is Figureoutable" Mindset

Work Challenge Assessment: Identify a recent or ongoing challenge in your professional life. Write down the details of this challenge, including the specific obstacles and your initial feelings about it.

Mindset Shift: Apply the "Everything is Figureoutable" mindset to the challenge you've identified. Write a statement that encapsulates this mindset and emphasizes your belief in your ability to find solutions. Repeat this statement whenever you face the challenge.

Resource Utilization: List the resources, knowledge, or skills you have at your disposal to address the challenge. Write down how you can leverage these resources to create solutions and overcome the obstacle.

Lesson 2:

Embracing Challenges for Growth

Challenge and Growth Reflection: Think about a significant challenge or setback you've encountered in your professional life. Write about the lessons you learned from that experience and how it contributed to your growth and development.

_____

_____

_____

_____

_____

_____

_____

_____

_____

_____

_____

_____

_____

_____

_____

_____

_____

_____

_____

_____

_____

_____

_____

_____

_____

_____

_____

_____

Challenge-Opportunity Matrix: Create a matrix where you categorize current work challenges as either "Obstacles" or "Opportunities." Write down your strategies for turning obstacles into opportunities for personal and professional growth.

Growth Action Plan: Choose one specific area where you'd like to further develop your skills or expertise. Write down a plan that includes actionable steps, resources, and a timeline for achieving growth in this area. Emphasize how challenges will be a part of this growth process.

_____

_____

_____

_____

_____

_____

_____

_____

_____

_____

_____

_____

_____

_____

_____

_____

_____

_____

_____

_____

_____

_____

_____

_____

_____

_____

_____

Lesson 3:

Problem-Solving for Career Value

Value Creation Analysis: Write a list of challenges or problems you've recently solved at work. Include the outcomes or value generated from your problem-solving efforts. Reflect on how these solutions contributed to your career advancement or the success of your team.

Future Problem-Solving Goals: Outline your career aspirations and goals. Write down the types of challenges or problems you anticipate encountering as you progress. Develop a proactive plan for how you will approach and solve these future challenges.

Collaborative Problem-Solving: Identify a colleague or team member with whom you can collaborate on a work challenge. Write down the specific challenge and how you plan to work together to find a solution. Collaboration often enhances problem-solving and creates value for both individuals and the organization.

Chapter 11:
Everything is Figureoutable in Love

Lesson 1:

Improving Relationships with Attitude and Effort.

Relationship Assessment: Reflect on a significant relationship in your life, whether it's with a partner, family member, or friend. Write down the current state of this relationship, including any challenges or issues you've encountered.

Attitude Shift: Apply the "Everything is Figureoutable" mindset to the relationship you've assessed. Write a statement that reflects your commitment to improving this relationship through a positive attitude and effort. Use this statement as a reminder when facing challenges.

_____

_____

_____

_____

_____

_____

_____

_____

_____

_____

_____

_____

_____

_____

_____

_____

_____

_____

_____

_____

_____

_____

_____

_____

Action Plan for Improvement: List specific actions or behaviors you can implement to enhance the relationship. Write down how you can improve communication, understanding, or empathy. Commit to taking these actions consistently.

_____

_____

_____

_____

_____

_____

_____

_____

_____

_____

_____

_____

_____

_____

_____

_____

_____

_____

_____

_____

_____

_____

_____

_____

Lesson 2:

Communication, Empathy, and Understanding in Relationships

Communication Reflection: Think about a recent communication challenge you faced in a relationship. Write down the details of the situation and how it was handled. Reflect on how improved communication could have positively influenced the outcome.

Empathy and Understanding Inventory: Create an inventory of your empathetic and understanding qualities. Write down instances where you've demonstrated empathy and understanding in your relationships. Identify areas where you can further develop these qualities.

_____

_____

_____

_____

_____

_____

_____

_____

_____

_____

_____

_____

_____

_____

_____

_____

_____

_____

_____

_____

_____

_____

Empathy Practice: Choose a relationship where you'd like to enhance empathy and understanding. Write down a specific scenario or conversation you anticipate having with the person. Develop strategies for actively listening, showing empathy, and demonstrating understanding during this interaction.

Lesson 3:

Applying Principles for Healthy, Loving Connections

Healthy Connection Goals: Write down your goals for fostering healthy, loving connections in your relationships. Include the qualities and dynamics you wish to cultivate in your interactions with others.

_____

_____

_____

_____

_____

_____

_____

_____

_____

_____

_____

_____

_____

_____

_____

_____

_____

_____

_____

_____

_____

_____

_____

_____

_____

Principles Application Plan: List the principles from the book that you believe will have the most significant impact on your relationships (e.g., "Everything is Figureoutable," "Communicate with Empathy"). Write down how you will apply these principles in your relationships.

_____

_____

_____

_____

_____

_____

_____

_____

_____

_____

_____

_____

_____

_____

_____

_____

_____

_____

_____

_____

_____

_____

_____

_____

_____

_____

Feedback and Growth: Select a trusted individual from one of your relationships and ask for their feedback on how you can improve your connection. Write down their insights and suggestions. Develop an action plan to address any areas for growth they've identified.

Chapter 12:
Everything is Figureoutable with Health

Lesson 1:

Taking Responsibility for Your Health.

Health Self-Assessment: Reflect on your current state of health and well-being. Write down any areas where you feel you could improve, such as physical fitness, nutrition, stress management, or sleep quality.

_____

_____

_____

_____

_____

_____

_____

_____

_____

_____

_____

_____

_____

_____

_____

_____

_____

_____

_____

_____

_____

_____

_____

_____

_____

Personal Health Responsibility Statement: Create a statement that reflects your commitment to taking responsibility for your health. Write it in the first person, present tense (e.g., "I take full responsibility for my health and well-being"). Use this statement as a daily reminder of your dedication to your health.

Health Improvement Plan: Choose one aspect of your health that you'd like to focus on improving. Write down specific actions you can take to address this area, such as setting fitness goals, improving your diet, or incorporating stress-reduction practices.

Lesson 2:

Prioritizing Self-Care, Nutrition, and Fitness

Self-Care Evaluation: Assess your current self-care routine. Write down the self-care practices you currently engage in and those you may have neglected. Identify areas where you can enhance your self-care.

Nutrition and Fitness Goals: Set specific nutrition and fitness goals for yourself. Write down what you want to achieve in terms of diet, exercise, or overall wellness. Include timelines and measurable outcomes to track your progress.

_____

_____

_____

_____

_____

_____

_____

_____

_____

_____

_____

_____

_____

_____

_____

_____

_____

_____

_____

_____

_____

_____

_____

_____

Healthy Routine Development: Create a daily or weekly routine that incorporates self-care, nutrition, and fitness practices. Write down the activities, timing, and duration of each practice. Use this routine as a guide to prioritize your health.

_____

_____

_____

_____

_____

_____

_____

_____

_____

_____

_____

_____

_____

_____

_____

_____

_____

_____

_____

_____

_____

_____

_____

_____

_____

Lesson 3:

Problem-Solving Health Challenges

Health Challenge Assessment: Identify a specific health challenge or obstacle you're currently facing. Write down the details of this challenge, including symptoms, triggers, and any actions you've taken so far.

_____

_____

_____

_____

_____

_____

_____

_____

_____

_____

_____

_____

_____

_____

_____

_____

_____

_____

_____

_____

_____

_____

_____

_____

_____

_____

_____

Problem-Solving Plan: Apply problem-solving techniques to address your health challenge. Write down potential solutions, including lifestyle adjustments, medical consultations, or alternative therapies. Develop a step-by-step plan for implementing these solutions.

Health Challenge Journal: Start a "Health Challenge Journal" to document your journey in overcoming the identified health challenge. Write about your progress, setbacks, and the effectiveness of the solutions you've implemented. Use this journal to track your health improvements.

Chapter 13: Everything is Figure-outable with Money

Lesson 1:

Shifting Your Money Mindset

Current Money Beliefs: Reflect on your current beliefs and attitudes about money. Write down any negative or limiting beliefs you may have inherited or developed over time.

_____

_____

_____

_____

_____

_____

_____

_____

_____

_____

_____

_____

_____

_____

_____

_____

_____

_____

_____

_____

_____

_____

_____

_____

_____

_____

_____

_____

Abundance Mindset Statement: Create a statement that reflects your commitment to adopting an abundance mindset (e.g., "I believe in my ability to attract wealth and abundance into my life"). Write this statement down and use it as a daily affirmation to shift your mindset.

_____

_____

_____

_____

_____

_____

_____

_____

_____

_____

_____

_____

_____

_____

_____

_____

_____

_____

_____

_____

_____

_____

Money Vision Board: Collect images, quotes, or symbols that represent your financial goals and aspirations. Create a visual money vision board by arranging these items on a board or digitally. Write down the specific financial goals associated with each element on your vision board.

Lesson 2:

Wise Financial Management and Wealth Growth

Financial Assessment: Evaluate your current financial situation. Write down your income, expenses, savings, investments, and debts. Use this assessment as a baseline to track your financial progress.

_____

_____

_____

_____

_____

_____

_____

_____

_____

_____

_____

_____

_____

_____

_____

_____

_____

_____

_____

_____

_____

_____

_____

_____

_____

Wealth-Building Goals: Set clear wealth-building goals for yourself. Write down the specific financial milestones you want to achieve, such as paying off debt, saving for retirement, or investing in assets.

Financial Growth Plan: Develop a financial growth plan that outlines the steps you'll take to achieve your wealth-building goals. Write down strategies for budgeting, saving, investing, and increasing your income.

Lesson 3:

Overcoming Financial Obstacles with Determination

Identify Financial Challenges: Identify a significant financial challenge or obstacle you're currently facing. Write down the details of this challenge, including the factors contributing to it.

_____

_____

_____

_____

_____

_____

_____

_____

_____

_____

_____

_____

_____

_____

_____

_____

_____

_____

_____

_____

_____

_____

_____

_____

_____

_____

_____

_____

_____

Resourceful Solutions: Apply a resourceful mindset to tackle your financial challenge. Write down creative and practical solutions you can implement. Include any additional resources or support you may need.

_____
_____
_____
_____
_____
_____
_____
_____
_____
_____
_____
_____
_____
_____
_____
_____
_____
_____
_____
_____
_____
_____
_____
_____
_____

Progress Tracking: Create a system for tracking your progress in overcoming the financial obstacle. Write down key milestones and deadlines. Regularly update your progress and adjust your approach as needed.

Chapter 14: Everything is Figure-outable with Time

Lesson 1:

Effective Time Management.

Time Audit: Conduct a time audit of your typical day or week. Write down how you spend your time, including work, personal activities, and leisure. Identify time-wasting habits or distractions.

Priority Setting: List your top priorities in life, including both short-term and long-term goals. Write down how you currently allocate your time to these priorities and whether any adjustments are needed to align them.

Distraction Elimination Plan: Identify common distractions that hinder your productivity. Write down specific strategies for minimizing or eliminating these distractions, such as setting boundaries or using productivity tools.

Lesson 2:

Time as a Tool for Life Design

Life Vision Statement: Create a vision statement for the life you want to create. Write down your aspirations, goals, and the values that guide your decisions. Use this statement as a foundation for shaping your use of time.

_____

_____

_____

_____

_____

_____

_____

_____

_____

_____

_____

_____

_____

_____

_____

_____

_____

_____

_____

_____

_____

_____

_____

_____

_____

_____

Time Allocation Plan: Develop a time allocation plan that aligns with your life vision. Write down how you intend to distribute your time among various life areas, such as career, relationships, personal development, and leisure.

_____
_____
_____
_____
_____
_____
_____
_____
_____
_____
_____
_____
_____
_____
_____
_____
_____
_____
_____
_____
_____
_____
_____
_____

Time Investment Analysis: Reflect on how you currently invest your time. Write down which activities or commitments contribute positively to your life vision and which ones may need adjustments or elimination.

Lesson 3:

Balancing Productivity and Self-Care

Productive Routine Creation: Outline a daily or weekly productive routine that includes focused work time, breaks, and self-care activities. Write down the specific tasks or activities you'll engage in during each part of the routine.

_____

_____

_____

_____

_____

_____

_____

_____

_____

_____

_____

_____

_____

_____

_____

_____

_____

_____

_____

_____

_____

_____

_____

Self-Care Commitment: Write a self-care commitment statement that emphasizes the importance of balancing productivity with self-care and relaxation (e.g., "I prioritize self-care to maintain balance and well-being"). Use this statement as a reminder to honor your self-care needs.

Weekly Reflection: At the end of each week, reflect on your time management and self-care practices. Write about what went well and areas where you can improve. Use this reflection to refine your time management strategies for the following week.

_____

_____

_____

_____

_____

_____

_____

_____

_____

_____

_____

_____

_____

_____

_____

_____

_____

_____

_____

_____

_____

_____

_____

_____

Made in United States
North Haven, CT
24 November 2024

60865337R00095